MW01243063

DIARY OF A DESERT TRAIL
1890 Cattle Drive from Arizona to California

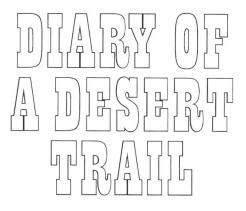

DIARY OF A DESERT TRAIL

1890 Cattle Drive
from Arizona to California

By Edward L. Vail

Introduction by Alison Bunting

EMPIRE RANCH FOUNDATION

Copyright © 2016 by Empire Ranch Foundation

ISBN 978-0-692-76355-1
Library of Congress Control Number: 2016952325

Published by Empire Ranch Foundation
Printed in the United States of America

Cover photos:
  *Edward L. Vail, ca. 1890. ERF photo archives: A455-1c, courtesy of Dusty Vail
    Ingram & Julia S. Ruch.*
  *Empire Ranch cattle, ca. 1920. ERF photo archives: A122-2a, courtesy of Dusty
    Vail Ingram.*
  Diary and background: Shutterstock.com
Cover and interior design: *M. Urgo*

For further information contact:
  Empire Ranch Foundation
  P. O. Box 842
  Sonoita, AZ 85637
  (888) 364-2829
  www.empireranchfoundation.org

Introduction

The Empire Ranch was founded in August of 1876 when Walter L. Vail and Herbert R. Hislop purchased a 160-acre ranch from Edward Nye Fish and Simon Silverberg for $2,000. Located north of present day Sonoita the ranch became one of the largest cattle ranches in southeastern Arizona.

Diary of a Desert Trail documents a significant event in Empire Ranch and southwestern history. Over 125 years ago, "the Empire Ranch led and won an early customer boycott challenging the powerful Southern Pacific Railroad. When a long drought hit Arizona hard in the late 1880's, Empire Ranch owners Walter Vail and C.W. Gates leased California pastures and shipped increasing numbers of their cattle there to fatten. Then, in the fall of 1889, on top of depressed cattle prices and despite loud protests from ranchers, the Southern Pacific Railroad, the only railroad in Arizona at that time, raised cattle freight rates by 25 percent to certain points in California. To defy the railroad rate increase, Tom Turner, foreman of the Empire Ranch, and Vail's brother Edward (known as "Ned" or "Tio"), volunteered to drive 900 steers overland to the Warner Ranch near San Diego."[1]

The drive began on January 29, 1890 and ended two months and ten days later. In addition to Edward Vail and Tom Turner the men who participated in the drive included "six Mexican cowboys from the ranch and a Chinese cook." We have been able to document the full names of

---

1 Browning, Sinclair. Empire Ranch v. Southern Pacific Railroad, 1890. Empire Ranch Foundation News, 2004 5(2):3-4.

five of the vaqueros: Chapo Miranda, José Blás P. López, George E. López, Néstor Gracia, and Jesús Elias, and the cook, Jong "John" Tong.

In 1922 Edward Vail shared the colorful story of the cattle drive, which he recorded in his diary, through a series of articles in the *Arizona Daily Star*. On the occasion of the 140th anniversary of the founding of the Empire Ranch we are pleased to republish the *Diary of a Desert Trail*, illustrated by photos from the Empire Ranch Foundation archives and other library collections. The text which follows was written by Edward Vail, the subheadings, editorial clarifications, drawings, and photos have been added for this publication.

Alison Bunting
Historian/Archivist
Empire Ranch Foundation
2016

DIARY OF A DESERT TRAIL

By Edward L. Vail

The Decision to Challenge the Rate Increase

The idea of driving a herd of cattle across southern Arizona to California was by no means an original one. After the gold discovery in California many emigrants crossed southern Arizona and the Colorado desert to San Diego, California with oxen and mule teams.

In the sixties and early seventies [1860s and 1870s], cattle became scarcer on the big ranches in California and many herds were driven over the southern trail. This route came through Tucson, led to the northwest to the Gila River, then followed that river to Yuma and from that point crossed the Colorado River to the more dangerous desert beyond.

It must be remembered that the early cattle drivers and emigrants who took the southern trail to the Pacific coast had to be prepared at times to defend themselves, their horses and cattle from the wily Apaches along the trail through New Mexico and Arizona as well as from the Yuma, who were not always friendly in those days.

Some years after, when the old Butterfield stages were still running, graves might be seen at many of the stations and along the trail with the simple inscription cut on a simple board, "Killed by the Indians."

In 1880 the Southern Pacific Railroad reached Tucson. It was several years after that, however, before there were any surplus cattle in Arizona to be shipped out. Walter L. Vail and C. W. Gates, then the owners of the Empire Ranch in Pima County, were among the first to use the railroad and up to 1889 had probably shipped as many as any other of the large ranches in Arizona.

In the fall of that year, the S. P. Company concluded that the cattlemen in southern Arizona would stand a freight raise, so they accordingly increased the rate to certain California points about 25 per cent. Cattle were low in price, and hard to sell at that time, especially stock cattle. A vigorous protest was made by the ranchmen – on the ground that the cattle in question were not beef, but young steers that had to be grown and fattened after reaching the California ranches before the owners could expect to get any return for them.

The railroad officials in San Francisco decided however, that they would make no reduction, probably thinking that the ranchers would be compelled to accept the new rate or keep their cattle in Arizona and then ship them over the only railroad there was in the country at this time.

The owners of the Empire Ranch, after considering the matter, decided to drive a herd of steers from the Empire Ranch to the Warner Ranch near San Diego. Tom Turner, foreman of the Empire Ranch, had worked on the trail from southern Texas to Dodge City, Kansas, when he was a boy and he and I decided that if men drove cattle from Texas to California 15 or 20 years before, and fought Indians nearly all the way, we could do it again.

So we told my brother, Mr. Walter Vail, that if he would take a chance on our losing the cattle, we would do our best to reach the destination safely. The herd was gathered and ready to start the latter part of January 1890. We had six Mexican cowboys from the ranch and a Chinese cook, whom we called John, who had worked for us for some time. He had cooked on many a roundup and could drive a four-horse team, brand a calf, or make a fair cowhand if necessary.

Start of the Cattle Drive— Empire Ranch to Southeast of Tucson

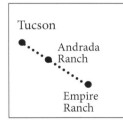

We left the ranch the 29th of January and after watering and camping at Andrada's that night, we drove on and found a dry camp on the desert about 15 miles southeast of Tucson. Our cattle were still steers: there were over 900 in the bunch and as most of the big ones had been gathered in the mountains, they were very wild and none of them had been handled on the trail before.

The part of the desert where we made camp was covered with chollas, a cactus that has more thorns per square inch than anything that grows in Arizona. Cowboys say that if you ride close to a cholla, it will reach out and grab you or your horse, and as the thorns are barbed it is very difficult to get them out of your flesh. They also leave a very painful wound.

About midnight, our cattle made a run and in trying to hold them, cattle, horses, and men got pretty badly mixed up in the chollas. A cholla under a horse's belly is probably not the most comfortable thing in the world. Consequently we had our hands full riding bucking horses and trying to quiet a lot of wild steers at the same time.

Most of the night was devoted in picking out thorns, and therefore none of us slept much. It was fortunate that we did not lose any cattle as they were not yet off the range, and any that escaped would have lost no time in getting back to their usual haunts, which might have been miles from our last camp.

Cattle and horses raised on the open range generally stay pretty close to the location where they are raised; they may change at certain seasons on account of better grass or early rains to another part of the range, but they usually return on their own accord, if well located, to their old stamping ground. Also, they have their own companions as running mates. It is no uncommon thing to see a cow, or even an old bull, watching a lot of very young calves whose mothers have gone to water. The guardian will protect all the little calves from coyotes, dogs, or any other enemy until their mothers return.

On to Tucson

With breakfast before daylight our cattle were headed toward Tucson and "yours truly" rode on ahead to buy a new chuck wagon and have it loaded with provisions and ready for the road. I had two 40-gallon water barrels rigged up, one on each side. John, the cook, came into town after breakfast and exchanged his old chuck wagon for the new one.

Our camp that night was to be on the Rillito Creek, just below Fort Lowell, about eight miles northeast of Tucson. We drove the cattle east of Tucson, past the present site of the University of Arizona and over what is the "north side" now, the best residence section of the city. At that time, the foundation of the University's first building was just being laid and it was about a mile from there to the nearest house in town. The surrounding country was covered in greasewood (creosote bush). A photographer from Tucson took a shot at our herd from the foundations of the University, but as I never saw any of the pictures, I think they must have been a failure. That night after we had watered the cattle in the Rillito, they were very restless and hungry and it kept us busy to hold them. The country was full of brush and we had to round them up to keep from losing them.

Tucson to Maricopa

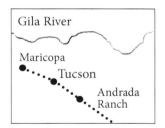

We followed the general directions of the S. P. railroad. The watering places were from 15 to 20 miles apart until we reached Maricopa, but several times we had to water in corrals. Many of our cattle were wild and had never been in a corral before and I am sure many of them did not drink at all.

That night we camped between Casa Grande and Maricopa. Turner and I concluded we would try to get a good night's sleep for once. We had been sleeping with all our clothes on and our horses ready saddled near us every night since we left the ranch, but as the cattle had been more quiet than usual for several nights past, we concluded to take off our outside clothes and get a more refreshing sleep. Sometime near midnight I awoke and was surprised to find we were in the middle of the herd and a lot of steers were lying down all around us. I awoke Tom quietly and asked him what he thought of our location. He answered, "The only thing to do is keep quiet. The boys know we are here and will work the cattle away from us as soon as they can do so safely. If the brutes don't get scared we will be all right."

I knew it was the only thing to do, but was a little nervous, nevertheless, and every time I heard a steer move or take a long breath it made me more so. The boys moved the cattle away from us a short distance, and not long after we had the worst stampede of the whole trip. Tom and I jumped on our horses without stopping to dress and we finally got most of the steers together, but as it was still very dark we could not tell whether we had them all or not. As soon as we had the cattle quieted, we made a fire and put on our clothes. We were nearly frozen.

I have rounded up cattle at all seasons of the year, but never before in my night clothes in the early part of February and at midnight. To make it worse, the country was full of washes and holes and "Billito", Tom's horse, fell down, but when he got up without his rider, he commenced to herd the cattle on his own account by running around them and pushing the stragglers in.

As soon as it was daylight, we counted the herd and found we were short about 150 head; we missed a good many of the big mountain steers that we remembered as the wildest of the bunch. We soon found their trail going north and from their tracks could easily tell that they were on the run. We must have traveled eight or ten miles before we caught sight of them and they were still on the trot. We were then on the Pima Indian Reservation near the Gila River. The Indians were on the hills all around us and they made some objections to our driving the cattle back, but we paid no attention to them and took the bunch back to our last night's camp where the rest of the boys were holding the main herd.

Which Route to Take from Maricopa?

The next day we reached Maricopa. At this point there was a choice of two routes; one went north and then followed the Gila River, which makes a big bend to the north here. This route would give us plenty of water, but would be much the longest. The other way was to follow the old stage road along the S. P. railroad to a place near Gila Station and then drop down on the river. This meant a drive of 50 miles without water, but was about half as far as the other and gave us a chance to find a little more grass for our cattle, as well as our horses which needed it badly. As we expected, our trail ran through a very poor country to find grass or other feed for either horses or cattle. We had two horses to each man and a few extra. In case some died or went lame. Although on a large cattle ranch each cowboy has 10 or 15 horses, we took as few as possible with us, because of the scarcity of grass.

We hauled barley in our chuck wagon and fed all our horses twice a day. We had several young saddle mules and some of them were very *bronco* when we left the ranch, but became gentle soon, especially about feeding time. There was one little roan mule in particular that was wild as a hawk when we started, but soon got acquainted with John the Cook, and came to the wagon for pieces of bread. There was also a little brown yearling steer the boys called "Brownie" and said he was *muy valiente* (very brave) because he always travelled with the leaders of the herd when we were on the move.

When camp was made, "Brownie" would pay us a visit and eat as many scraps he could get, as well as any barley or corn the horses had spilled. The boys agreed that if "Brownie" gave out, we should put him in the chuck wagon and haul him to California.

I must say a few words about our Mexican cowboys; most of them were very good hands and some of them as fine ropers as I have ever seen. They knew how to handle cattle on a ranch and in a roundup. Driving cattle a few miles to a corral, or throwing them together in a rodeo is a very different thing however, from driving them 500 miles on the desert with water 50 miles apart in some places. Practically the only trouble we had with our men was to keep them from driving too fast. Travelling behind a herd, day after day, on a dusty trail is certainly a monotonous job, but we knew the only possible way we could expect to reach the Warner Ranch with our cattle alive, was to hurry them only when it was necessary.

After the cattle got used to the trail at night we usually had two of them on guard at a time. When camp was made, the first guard had supper and was relieved in four hours by the men who, in their turn, went off duty when the last guard went on about 2 a.m. As soon as it was light, the latter would start the cattle grazing on the direction we were traveling, and most of the day our steers wandered along, browsing on the mesquite, sage, and sometimes a little grass. Even traveling that way they did not get much to eat and I often wondered what kept them alive. When we reached Maricopa, the only water we found for our cattle was in a ditch near the railroad and it was probably an over-flow from the water tank or from the recent rain. We finally got all the cattle and horses watered and let them rest awhile.

Maricopa to Gila Bend

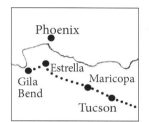

In the afternoon we hit the trail for Gila Bend, and driving out slowly about ten miles on the old stage road riding the north side of the railroad, we made a late camp for the night. The next afternoon we reached Estrella, which is at the head of a valley which would be rather pretty if it were not so dry. There are desert mountains on each side and south of the little station a mountain higher than the rest forms a rincon. Tom concluded we would turn the cattle loose that night by grazing them in the direction of that mountain and then guarding them only on the lower side, thus giving them a chance to lie down whenever they liked, or to eat any grass or weeds they could find. I remember it was a beautiful night and not very cold. In the moonlight, I could see the cattle scattered around on the hills and could hear the boys singing their Spanish songs as they rode back and forth on guard. I am not sure whether cattle are fond of music or not, but I think where they are held on a bed ground at night, they seem better contented and are less excitable when the men on guard sing or whistle. This custom is so common on

15

the trail that I have often heard one cowpuncher ask another how they held their cattle on a roundup. The other would reply, "Oh, we had to sing to them!"

There is one thing that may seem funny now, but it did not seem so at that time. When we commenced making dry camps and using the water from the barrels on our wagon, we found it had a very disagreeable taste. I supposed that the barrels I had bought in Tucson had been used for whiskey or wine, a flavor to which I do not think a cowboy would seriously object, but they proved to be old sauerkraut barrels! We had no chance to clean them thoroughly until we got to the river. Then I took the heads off and cleaned out all the kraut and soaked them in the river. The next day we drove the cattle about ten miles down the winding canyon along the railroad toward Gila, and made our third dry camp west of Maricopa. Before leaving Estrella, I begged water enough from the section foreman there to water our wagon team. Both my brother and I had very warm friends among the railroad men of the Tucson division, and often when driving or holding our cattle along the track, the conductor and trainmen would wave their caps to us from the passing train, and sometimes throw us a late newspaper.

We expected to reach Gila Bend on the river the next evening and started the cattle early in the morning toward the Gila Valley. We had reached a point which was clear of the hills on a big flat that gradually sloped toward the river; suddenly, the big steers in the lead threw up their heads and commenced to sniff the breeze, which happened to be blowing from the river, while a weird sound like a sigh or moan seemed to come from the entire herd. I had been driving cattle for many years then, but had never heard them make that noise before. They were very thirsty and had suddenly smelled water! They had been dragging along as if it was hard work even to walk, but in a minute they were on the dead run. Every man but one was in front, beating the head cattle over the heads with coats and slickers trying to check them, as we feared they would run themselves to death before the water was reached. Close to the river we turned them loose, or rather they made us get out of their way.

Then we found that one of our men had been caught in the rush of the cattle. They had outrun his already tired horse, but he was doing his best to keep the horse on his feet. If his horse had fallen with him the cattle would probably have trampled the man to death. Here, several of our men showed courage and quick action. Pushing their horses against one side of the string of cattle that were rushing towards their companion, they pressed it to the other side far enough to release him from his dangerous position.

The lead steers plunged into the Gila River like fish hawks, drinking as they swam and crossing to the other side. The drags (or slow cattle) must have been at least three miles behind us when the first steers reached the river and, after watering our horses, which we did carefully, some of the cowboys went back to help the man we had left behind to follow them in.

Gila Bend to Yuma

We grazed our cattle and horses at Gila Bend for several days and gave them a chance to rest. Turner or I generally did some scouting ahead to find a good watering place for

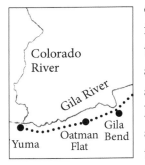

our cattle and the next day's camp. We found a trail along the south side of the river, about 30 feet above it, with a steep mountain on the other side and only wide enough for a man on horseback to pass. We followed it for about a mile and it brought us out on the Oatman Flat, a nice piece of land named for the Oatman family, the members of which were killed there by the Apaches in 1850. The way of reaching this place was over a very rocky mountain road and much longer. We decide to drive the cattle over the trail by the river. The cattle were started in that direction with a rider leading them as usual. As soon as we had a few lead steers on the narrow trail the others followed like sheep and all reached Oatman safely. So many cattle walking single file was an unusual sight. The wagon had to go by the longer road. At the Oatman Flat we met the Jourdan family, with whom we were acquainted. Turner and I spent the evening very pleasantly at their house. The Jourdans were doing some farming and also had cattle. Gila Bend is about half way between Tucson to Yuma, and from what I saw of the Gila Valley I did not think much of it as a cattle country. We had some trouble with quicksand when watering cattle in the river. If a steer got stuck in the sand the only way to get him out was to wade in and pull out one leg at a time and then tramp the sand around that leg (this gets the water out of the sand which holds it in suspension). When all the legs were free we would turn the animal on its side and haul it to the bank with our reatas.

Continued on page 25

Photos • Diary of a Desert Trail

Men who drove 900 cattle to California in 1890 in the Empire Ranch House corral. Left to right: Severo "Chappo" Miranda, José Blás P. López, George E. López, Néstor Gracia, Francisco (last name unknown), ranch foreman Tom Turner, Jesús Elias, Rafael (last name unknown), and Edward L. Vail (far right). Not pictured, cook Jong "John" Tong. Arizona Historical Society (Photograph #090317).

Day 3 of the cattle drive. They made camp at the Rillito Creek just below Ft. Lowell, about 8 miles northeast of Tucson, AZ. ERF photo archives: A530-07, courtesy of Whitney Wilkinson.

Left: Edward "Ned" Vail ca. 1890. ERF photo archives: A455-1c, courtesy of Dusty Vail Ingram, Julia S. Ruch.

Right: Tom Turner, Empire Ranch foreman, ca. 1900. ERF photo archives A537-041, courtesy of Gary Turner.

Walter L. Vail, founder of the Empire Ranch, 1894. ERF photo archives: A442-1, courtesy of Dusty Vail Ingram, Julia S. Ruch.

Home of vaquero Severo "Chappo" Miranda (on the ladder) with his family around him. Hadden McFadden, Empire Ranch foreman is on the left and Harry Heffner, Empire Ranch cowboy and later foreman, is on the right, 1890s. Special Collections, University of Arizona Libraries: Harry Heffner Empire Ranch photograph collection (MS 506, Box 3, N-659).

José Blás Lopéz (seated) with daughter Rosario Lopéz to his right at his home in Greaterville, AZ, 1899. His wife Maria Pallanes Lopéz is seated to his left, holding daughter Rita Lopéz with daughter Elena Lopéz standing to her right. Arnulfo Peña is standing at center rear. ERF photo archives: A537-021, courtesy of Edward Gardner.

Empire Ranch buildings and cattle, 1880s. ERF photo archives: A433-1, courtesy of Dusty Vail Ingram, Julia S. Ruch.

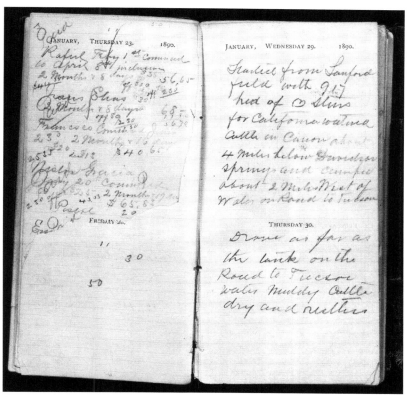

Edward Vail's diary entries for the first two days of the cattle drive. Special Collections, University of Arizona Libraries: Diary of Edward L. Vail (AZ271).

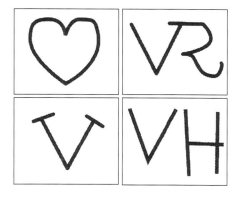

Empire Ranch brands used by the Vail family. ERF archives.

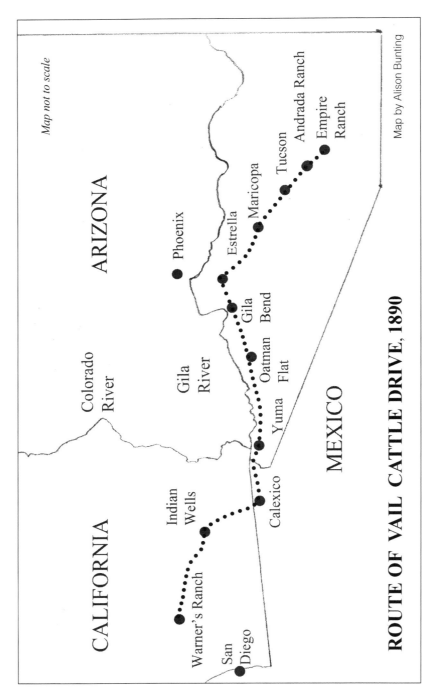

Map not to scale

Map by Alison Bunting

ROUTE OF VAIL CATTLE DRIVE, 1890

I never saw so many quail in my life as in that country. John the Cook would take my shotgun and kill a lot of them. At night when he called us to supper he would say, "All the boys come, plente quai to-night." He could not say quail.

There were very few incidents of particular interest on the trail down the Gila Valley to Yuma. One evening when we were ready to camp for the night John drove his team down on a little flat near the river where there were quite a number of willows and cottonwood trees. When Tom rode over and saw the place he told the Chinaman to hitch up his team and drive up on the higher ground near where the cattle were to be held that night. The cook said, "See what a pretty place this is Mr. Tom." Tom replied that it was pretty all right but too far from the cattle in case of trouble, and too far for the men to go in the night when the guards changed. The next morning when we awoke we heard a great roaring from the river. We lost no time riding over to the river to see what had happened. The Gila was a raging flood and the place John had picked out to camp was eight or ten feet under water. If we had slept there that night the men would have been the only survivors of our outfit. Afterwards we heard that the Walnut Grove dam, many miles away, had given way and quite a number of people were drowned in the valley below the dam. We were compelled to leave some of our cattle before we reached Yuma as there was scarcely any grass or weeds, and the mesquite and other forage had not yet budded out. Some steers died but most of them gave out and we turned them loose.

Resupplying Prior to Crossing the Colorado River

I kept a list of the cattle we left; I think there were about 25 or 30 before we reached Yuma. While we were at Gila Bend I went with the cook and his wagon to Gila station and bought barley for our horses and provisions. Before we reached Agua Caliente (hot springs) near Sentinel I rode on ahead as we heard there was a store at the springs and laid in another supply there. The hot springs are on the north side of the river, and as there was considerable water in the river there a man in a boat rowed me over. I took advantage of the opportunity and enjoyed a good bath in the warm water, which is truly wonderful. I doubt there is any better in the country. At that time the accommodations were very poor there for persons visiting the springs, especially for sick people.

About 30 miles from Yuma, Jim Knight and one of his cowboys met us — Knight was the foreman of the Warner Ranch and a cousin of Tom Turner's. He brought us saddle mules and horses and they were all fat. These were to take the place of some of the horses we had ridden so far. There was one of the most important things for us that Jim failed to do, however, — that was to find out if there was any water on the Colorado desert for our cattle and where it was. I think he said he only watered his horses once between Carrizo Creek and the Colorado River, a distance of over 100 miles and he knew of no other water out there. As we were then only about half way on our road to the Warner Ranch and the worst was yet to come, Knight's report did not cheer us much.

The mules Jim brought were young and unbroken and as stubborn as only a mule can be. It was hard to turn one around on a 10 acre lot. Two of our boys refused to ride them. We told them if they would go as far as Yuma we would pay for their fare back to Pantano, as that was the agreement we made with our men before leaving the ranch, but I think they were homesick and I could not blame them much. We paid them off and they took the next train for Tucson at the nearest station to our camp. Those mules had a surprise in store for them and I will admit it was new to me at that time. On the ranch when breaking colts we use either a hackamore or an American snaffle bit until they become well reined so that by pressing the rein on one side of the neck they will turn in the opposite direction. Tom took a piece of rope long enough to pass the middle of it over the saddle horn and each end through the ring of the bit in the mule's mouth. The ends of the rope were then fastened to the cinch rings of the saddle on either side. If one of those California mules got fresh and took it into his head to run through a mesquite thicket with you, all you had to do was pull hard enough and you could double his nose back to the saddle on either side as the rope ran freely through the rings in the bit which acted as pulleys. Before long those Warner mules were doing their share of the work which helped us very much on the next part of the trip.

Crossing the Colorado River

In a few days more we reached Yuma and camped on the Colorado River, about three miles southwest of the town. The river was rather high owing to an unusual amount of water flowing into it from the Gila which joins it on the north side of the town. The next day we let all of our cowboys go to town to buy some clothing, which some of them needed badly and we gave them free rein to enjoy themselves as they pleased. Of course they did not go all at one time as some had to stay and herd the cattle. Among the last of our men to get back to camp that night was Severo Miranda (Chappo). He was somewhat "lit up" and made a short speech to Tom Turner in Spanish, which translated amounted to this: "Mr. Tom, I am sorry that I am pretty full tonight, and you know that no matter what you tell me to do I am always ready and willing to do it – riding mean mules or anything else." Pa Chappa, as he is called now, commenced working at the Empire Ranch about 1880 and is still on the payroll. In February 1922, his grandson was buried in Tucson, a victim of the World War. He served in the U. S. Navy and contracted tuberculosis at that time.

Turner and I got a boat with an Indian to row it, and spent the day looking for the best place to swim the cattle. We rode two or three miles up and down the Colorado River and prodded the banks with poles to see how deep the quicksand was. We found it very bad, especially on the west bank where the cattle would land. Finally we found an island near the west bank of the river where the landing was better. The water was not very deep from the island, with a good landing on the other side. We then returned to the Arizona side of the river and found it was impossible to drive the cattle into the river there as the bank formed a 10-foot perpendicular wall above the water. We hired a lot of Yuma Indians with picks and shovels. They graded a road to the water. This work occupied a day or two. We were then ready to attempt taking the cattle across.

The herd had not been watered since the day before in order to make them thirsty. The current was very strong and the river very deep. We found it would be impossible for men on horseback to do anything in guiding the cattle across so we hired the Indians and three or four boats. We placed them so as to keep the cattle from drifting down stream. The idea was not to let them turn back for land so far down as to miss the island. We got the cattle strung out and traveling as they had on the trail with the big steers in the lead and men on each side to keep them in position to go down the grade which we had made to reach the river. Most of the large cattle reached the island all right. Then our troubles began!

Two or three hundred of the smaller steer got frightened as the current was too swift for them and they swam back to the Arizona side. About this time the sheriff from Yuma showed up and said he had orders from the district attorney to hold our cattle until we paid taxes on them in Yuma County. I told him I thought the district attorney was mistaken but we were too busy to find out just then. Cattle were scattered all along the river on the Arizona side and as they could not climb the banks and get out, many of them were in the water just hanging to the bank with their feet. We hired all the Indians we could get and with the help of our own men we pulled all excepting two or three of the cattle up that steep bank.

It was then about 10 o'clock at night. The Yuma Indians quit and they were hungry and tired. We did not doubt them a bit as we had eaten nothing since a breakfast before daylight. So we made it unanimous and all quit and went to Yuma. We were all terribly dirty so we went to the hotel at the depot, got a bath, some supper, a bed, and a deep sleep!

In the meantime here is the way we were situated. Our chuck wagon, cook and blankets were across the river; our 600 cattle were loose on the island in the river where we could not herd them; nearly 300 steers were loose in the thickest [brush] I have ever seen and on the Arizona side; and we were in the hands of the sheriff of Yuma county. The next morning Mr. C. W. Gates arrived on the train from Los Angeles. He went down with us to the scene of yesterday's operations. The first thing we did was to pull out the two steers we left clinging to the river bank. Then we told Mr. Gates that if he would take what men we could spare and start to gather the cattle we had turned loose in the brush that Tom and I would go over in a boat to the island and swim the cattle over to the California side of the river. Throwing our saddles into the boat leading the horses, swimming behind, we soon reached the island. The cattle seemed to be all right. We did not have any trouble in getting them over as we found the big steers could wade across, but most of the younger ones had to swim a short distance. When we got them all across we looked up the best place we could hold them and made camp.

When we got back to where we had left Mr. Gates we found him and Chappo on a boat along the river bank. Mr. Gates said, "Tom, you can never gather those cattle in that brush," and I admit it did not look possible. At that time Mr. Gates had only been a short time in the cattle business and never worked them on a range. So

Tom and I told Gates if he would go to Tucson and see his attorney about the tax matter we would gather the lost cattle if possible.

I forgot to say how our Chinese cook left for Pantano on the train soon after we arrived in Yuma. He said if he crossed the river he would never come back again. The day before he left he bought a large Colorado salmon alive from a Yuma Indian who had just caught it. John took the fish, which was over two foot long, up to Mr. Gondolfo's store and got permission to put it in a large galvanized water tank in the back yard. John said: "I am going to take that fish back to the Empire Ranch for Mrs. Vail."

When John went to get his fish the tank was full of water. So with permission from the owner the water was drawn off, but John could not wait for all of it to run out. When the water was about two feet deep he could see the fish and became so excited that he jumped in, clothes and all. I was watching him and it was quite a circus. He grabbed at that fish several times before he caught it; then his foot slipped and he rolled over in the bottom of the tank, but when he got up he had the fish. If anything, I think he was wetter than the fish, but he only said: "Mr. Ned, that fish pretty dam quick, but I catched him alitte."

John wrapped the fish in his slicker and was soon on his way to Pantano. When he arrived there in his anxiety to present the fish to Mrs. Vail in good condition he telephoned for a team to meet him.

Before Mr. Gates left Yuma he telegraphed my brother, who was at the Empire Ranch, that we were swimming the cattle and I was in trouble over the tax matter. When the message reached Pantano it was transmitted over the telephone to the ranch. The line was not working well and the only thing my brother could understand was, "Ned trouble, swimming river." He at once concluded that I had been drowned in the river. He saddled his fastest horse, "Lucero," and I am told he made the fastest time on record to Pantano. When he read the message and found the trouble was about taxes, he said: "That word never looked so good to me before."

At first we did not make much progress in gathering those steers. The brush was so thick we could not get through it on horseback. It was screw-bean, which does not grow high but the limbs are long and dropping on the ground and lying there between them arrow weed was as thick as hair on a dog and higher than a man's head. We found that we could run some of the steers out of the brush afoot by starting near the river and scaring them up to the open mesa as the brush only extends back a short distance from the river. After a few days the cattle commenced coming out themselves and we soon had quite a bunch together.

In the meantime, Mr. Frances J. Heney, who was at that time acting attorney for Vail & Gates at Tucson, decided our tax troubles as follows, viz. That the taxes had been paid on our cattle before they left the home ranch and that the cattle in transit were not subject to taxation any place in Arizona. Mr. Heney also advised the Yuma county attorney to read the Arizona statutes and let Pima county cattlemen alone. Then the sheriff's deputy wanted us to pay him for holding our cattle, but I told him we never hired him and as the sheriff put him there he had better collect from him. The deputy's name was Green. He had a livery stable in Yuma, where we had kept our horses ever since we arrived. He was a pretty good fellow. I think Mr. Gates was in favor of paying him, as we had worked him like one of our own men, holding the cattle. Tom and I were getting pretty sore by that time and said we would see that bunch of Yuma politicians in a hotter place than Yuma if there was before we would pay any of them a cent. After four or five days we had gathered most of the cattle on the Yuma side. Then I ordered cars and shipped them across the bridge there. We made a chute of an old wagon box and railroad ties and unloaded them. It would no doubt have been cheaper to have shipped our cattle across the bridge at $2.50 a carload but we did not like the idea of depending on the railroad in any way.

Crossing the "Great Colorado Desert"

We soon got all our cattle together on the California side and were ready to move. All were glad to get away from Yuma and take our chance on "The Great Colorado Desert," as it was then called. We followed the river and met a man named Carter, who had a small cattle ranch, from whom we bought half a beef that he had just killed. Our cattle were too poor for beef and while a beef was more than we could haul, and as the days were warm, we were afraid it would spoil before we could eat it.

Carter was said to know the desert well and I tried to hire him as a guide and offered him $20 a day to show us where the water was on the desert. He said he, "had not been out there for some time. Sometimes there was plenty of water out there and often no water as it depended entirely on whether there had been rain."

We decided that Mr. Carter was probably right about the water on the desert and what we saw afterwards confirmed that opinion. We did not travel very far down the river before we were overtaken by two young men with four or five very thin horses. They said their name was Fox, that they were brothers, and that they had been following us for some time and were anxious to cross the desert and heard we were driving the cattle across to California and asked if we could not give them a job to help drive our cattle.

Tom Turner told them we had plenty of help as the cattle were getting very gentle and we had all the men we needed. Tom and I then had a talk and we decided to let them go with us as they said they were afraid to cross the desert alone as they knew nothing about the country. We told them if they were willing to help us we would let them go along with us. Tom told them that they could turn their horses in the "Remuda" (loose horses) and he would let them ride some of our mules which came from the Warner Ranch.

We were close to the line of Lower California and soon after we crossed it we came to an Indian rancheria. I believe they were Cocopah Indians. The men wore breech cloths and the women wore aprons made out of the bark of willow trees. They were fine specimens of Indians, the men looking like athletes. I have been told that they came up from the Cocopah Mountains south of the desert to farm during the summer, raising mostly corn, pumpkins and melons, then during the winter migrating back to the mountains. We had not been around their camp long before we got a message from the chief who sent us word that we were on their land and had no right to pass through there with our cattle and that "all good people" who passed through gave them two steers.

We sent word to the chief by his messenger, who could speak Spanish, that we would have a conference with their chief, so the meeting was arranged and we went to the chief's home. After a parley in Spanish, we told the chief that we were considered "good people" where we came from but that we did not own the cattle we were driving, therefore we would have no right to give any of them away. We told him we would be glad if he would send one of his men to our chuck wagon to give him some sugar and coffee. We were sorry that we did not have much more to spare, but as we had a long way to go and no stores along the road where we could buy more, we could not give them more than we did.

We followed the old stage road down to where it left the river. I have forgotten the exact distance but it could not of have been over 20 miles. In this place there was quite a lagoon of water, so we camped there. Next day Tom and I followed the old road out into the desert looking for water for our next camp. I never saw so many rattlesnakes in my life as we did that day. They seemed to be of two varieties, the large ordinary diamondback and a little rattlesnake that we called "sidewinders," which has little horns over its eyes. We rode a good ways that day and came back to camp late quite discouraged as owing to the poor condition our cattle we were afraid of driving them a long distance without water. When we reached camp we were surprised to find several tents pitched close to us on the lagoon. We immediately inquired of our men as to who the people were. They did not know but thought they were engineers of some kind. Tom and I went over to see and introduced ourselves to the head man.

He proved to be D. K. Allen a civil engineer who told us he was making a preliminary survey for a railroad from Encinado [Ensenada], Lower California to Yuma and he had been out in the desert all winter. We then told him our anxiety about finding water and he assured us there was plenty of water on the desert and that the first water we would find was only 17 miles from our present camp. This he said was not sufficient for all our cattle, but further on about 10 miles just across the line near the boundary monument on New River there was quite a large charka [*charco* or water hole] in the channel of the New River which would probably water all the cattle for a week.

While we were at his camp the cook was preparing supper and we asked him what he was cooking. He said it was rattlesnake and he invited us to partake of it. We passed it along to all our crew who had called on Mr. Allen, as people were so scarce in that country they were as much interested in meeting someone as we were. The only man among us who tasted it was Jesus Maria Elias, who told us that when he was with General Crook as his chief trailer he had frequently eaten it. I knew Elias and his family well, but I never knew he was so celebrated a man as he really was.

I afterwards learned that he was the leader of the celebrated so-called "Camp Grant Massacre." He with William Orey [Oury], eight Americans, quite a number of Mexicans and a large number of Papago Indians marched over to the mouth of Aravaipa Canyon, which was right in sight of the old Camp Grant but then occupied by American troops and nearly exterminated that band of Apaches. They killed all but the children whom they brought to Tucson as prisoners. The cause of this expedition was the constant raids of the Apaches against the settlers on the San Pedro and Santa Cruz rivers. A full account of this interesting expedition can be found in the second volume of Farrish's [Thomas Edwin Farish] *History of Arizona*.

I found Mr. Allen to be a very interesting man who had traveled extensively throughout Old Mexico and was very much interested in everything that he saw in the wild parts of that country. He asked us if we had any beef that we could let him have as he had been eating rattlesnakes for some time as he had no other meat, we sent him over part of the beef we bought from Joe Carter. Mr. Allen was afterwards editor of a Yuma paper; I think it was the *Sentinel*. We asked him in regard to the trail across Carrizo Creek and showed him the maps of San Diego County, which then extended to the Colorado River. He marked out all the watering places that he knew about, the last one of which would bring us to within about 40 miles of Carrizo Creek. He also said he would send one of his own men who knew the country with us if we had any trouble finding the watering places and would send back for the man. He was very generous and did not expect any compensation for helping us.

The next afternoon we bid goodbye to Mr. Allen and the Colorado Valley and drove out 10 miles and camped for the night. The next morning early we were on our way and about afternoon reached the first watering place that Mr. Allen had referred to. After looking at it we decided we would only be able to water the weakest of the cattle. We had held the cattle back some distance from this water and Turner and I went ahead and looked at it as we were afraid the cattle would make a rush for the water. We cut our herd in two. As the stronger cattle were ahead on the road, we drove them on and let the weaker ones have the water.

Calexico and New River

About dark that night we reached the second watering place. This was near the New River stage station on the old overland road, but just across the line. This is the present site of the town of Calexico. We were quite pleased at the looks of what we could see of the country thereabouts. The mesquite was beginning to bud out with plenty of old grass around. The grass is commonly called *guayella*. The green shoots grow out of the old roots with a head like Timothy [grass]. Also there was a great deal of what cattlemen call the "careless-weed." All the cattle ate heartily and enjoyed their first good feed for some days. We concluded to stay for several days. And give our cattle a chance to rest.

The next day Turner and I thought we would take a ride over to Indian Wells, the next watering place. We easily found the water and the ruins of the old stage station. This is near what is called Signal Mountain, a very peculiar peak, the only one I saw in the desert as the country all around is very level. The water at Indian Wells was in a round basin with mesquite trees growing all around it. While we were there Turner's horse was taken sick and seemed to be in considerable pain. We laid down under a tree to rest. I soon fell asleep. Some kind of bird cried over my head and made a noise like a rattler.

Turner afterwards told me it was a catbird. I don't know what it was, but at the time I nearly jumped into the water. As it was getting late we concluded we had better be getting back to camp. We decided to leave Turner's horse there so we tied him up. I was riding a little horse which although small proved to have plenty of endurance. We put both our saddles on my horse one on top of the other. We took turns riding. One would ride ahead, then dismount and walk, leaving the horse for the one on foot to catch up to and ride. Alternating this way we had no difficulty in getting back to camp.

While camping at New River we found many things of interest. Most of the country was covered in very small snail shells. They were so small that I first took them to be seeds of some weed. However, they were perfect shells although not larger than the size of the head of a pin. I gathered some of them as curios. In exploring around we found many signs of cattle herds which had crossed the desert years before. At one place, I remember well, we found where the cattle had been bedded for the night and the tracks of the cattle, horses and wagon were distinct. The soil was a sort of heavy clay, which must have been wet when the cattle were there. I should judge from the size of the bed ground and in front the bones of cattle that we found scattered around there, (some of the skeletons being complete) that it was quite a herd. We followed the wagon tracks a short distance and found mesquite trees growing up between wagon tracks.

We sat on our horses reading the story of the trail those old cowboys had left in the desert spaces. We could see from the number of cattle they lost the night they camped there, that their cattle were in bad shape. I should judge that the tracks had been made 20 years before as the trees were probably that old by their size, since trees make a slow growth on the desert.

Later we found a human skull which we put in the wagon and carried the rest of the way with us. We also found a wrecked wagon with the axle broken apparently abandoned. Afterwards I hear that it probably belonged to some people who had perished in the desert. I believe if the history of that desert could be written it would prove very interesting reading for anyone who cared for real tragedy.

From our camp at New River we drove to Indian Wells, north of Signal Mountain. Late the next day we started for Carrizo Creek which makes the western boundary of the desert. This was the longest drive without water we had to make crossing the Colorado Desert. I think it was 40 miles. Our cattle had done well while camped at New River as there was more pasture for them there than at any place on the trail since we left the Empire Ranch. The country was open so we loose herded them. Strange to say the only steers we lost on the desert were drowned in the *charco* at New River. The reader may remember we turned our cattle loose the night we arrived there. The two steers were young and very weak and probably got their feet fast in the mud in the middle of the pool. We drove frequently at night as the days were warm on the desert. We hung a lantern on the tall board of our wagon and our lead steers would follow it like soldiers. Before we reached Yuma only one man was necessary on guard so we changed every three hours which gave the men more sleep, but it was rather a lonesome job for the fellow that had to watch the cattle.

The road had a decided grade as it approached the mountains and there was much heavy sand most of the way which made it very tiresome. I am not quite sure how long we were making that part of the drive, as we had to rest the cattle every few hours. When we reached Carrizo we found a shallow stream of water in a wash the banks of which were white with alkali. Not only the stream but the hills, barren of all vegetation, were full of the same substance. I never saw a more desolate place in my life. In all of Arizona there is nothing to compare with it that I know of.

The next morning the cattle were scattered up and down the creek most of them lying down and a few of them eating what little salt grass they could find. They had come through all right from our last camp, except one young steer that could not get up. We tried to lift him on his feet but he could not stand so I told the boys I was going out to see if I could find bunch grass along the hills and the youngest of the Fox brothers offered to go with me. He was a good looking young man, nearly six feet tall and about 20 years old I should think. His brother was a rather short and heavily built. These boys had worked cheerfully since they met us and were on good terms with all our men.

The Sheriff's Unexpected Arrival

Young Fox and I found some grass and brought it to the sick steer. Fox was a pleasant young fellow and said that Tom Turner had offered to give them work on the Empire Ranch if they would go back there with our men. A little later I was surprised to see a carriage with four men in it coming toward our camp from the west. One of the men beckoned to me and I walked over to see what they wanted and who they were. They were the first people we had seen since we left the Colorado River, about a hundred miles back. He said he was a sheriff from Arizona and as he spoke I recognized him. He then asked if we had two Americans with us who joined us near Yuma, and I replied that we had. Then he introduced me to the other three men, one of whom was his deputy and the other, his driver, who was from Temecula, California, and I think he said a deputy sheriff there. The fourth man, the sheriff told me came with him from Arizona and was the owner of some horses which he said the Fox boys had stolen from his ranch. The sheriff then told me that he and his deputy had followed the Fox brothers all the way to Yuma and then they had followed our trail after the boys until we crossed the line. They then returned to Yuma and took the train for California, as he could not go into Mexico.

As nearly as I remember I said: "Sheriff, you know the reputation of our outfit; it has never protected a horse thief and has always tried to assist an officer in the discharge of his duty." I also told the sheriff that the boys had done the best they could to help us in crossing the desert and that I was sorry to hear they were in trouble. I felt it was my duty to tell him that the boys were well armed and quick with a gun. "You have plenty of men to take them," I said. "Be careful. I don't want anybody hurt." The sheriff answered, "If they ask you anything, tell them that we are mining men going out to look at a mine."

I knew if the boys were sure that the men were officers there would be bloodshed at once. It was a very unpleasant position for me as I really felt a good deal of sympathy for the brothers and I knew them to be young and reckless. The older one came to me and said, "Who are those men and what do they want?"

I had to tell him what the sheriff told me to say: viz, that they said they were mining men out to look at a mine near there. I could see he was not satisfied and was still anxiously watching the sheriff's party. The newcomers then said they were hungry and I told the man who was cooking to get them something to eat. While they were eating they talked about the mine they were going out to see and I think the boys were less suspicious of them.

Very soon after I was standing on one side of the chuck wagon, the elder brother was leaning against the back and his brother near the front wheel on the opposite side of the wagon from me. Suddenly I heard a scuffle and when I looked up I saw the sheriff and another man grab the elder boy and take his gun. His deputy and assistant were holding his brother on the other side of the wagon. They had quite a struggle and young Fox pulled away from them, ran around the wagon past me with the deputy in pursuit. He ran about a hundred yards up a sandy gulch and the deputy was quite close to the boy when he raised his gun and fired. Young Fox dropped and never moved again. I was close behind the deputy as I had followed them. When the latter turned toward me with his six-shooter still smoking and he was wiping it with his handkerchief, "I hated to do it," he said, "but you have to sometimes."

I was angry and shocked at his act, as I had never seen a man shot in the back before. I then saw the other Fox boy walking toward his brother's body, which was still lying on the ground. The officers who had him handcuffed tried to detain him, but he said, "Shoot me if you like, but I am going to my brother." He walked over to where the body lay and looked at it. Then he asked me if we would bury his brother and I told him he could depend on us to do so.

Then I told the sheriff there was no excuse for killing the boy as he could not get away in that kind of country. He replied that he was very sorry about what had happened but said, "You know, Vail, that I got my man without killing him, and that it was impossible for me to prevent it, as I had my hands full with the other fellow at the time."

Tom Turner was not in camp when this happened as he had gone out around the cattle. The sheriff and his posse left shortly after and took their prisoner with them, but they left the body of young Fox lying on the ground where he fell. We dug a grave and, wrapping the young man's body in his blanket, buried him near the place where he fell. It was the best we could do. I saw a man in Tucson last week who told me he was at Carrizo Creek a few years ago where he saw the grave which had a marker with the inscription, "Murdered."

Carrizo Creek to Warner Ranch

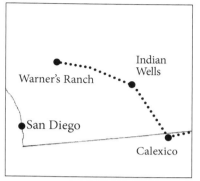

We were glad to leave Carrizo the next morning and be on the way to Warner Ranch. The country was dry and barren until we reached Vallecinto [Vallecito] creek, which is in a pretty little valley with some green grass growing in it. Between there and Warner, we passed the San Felipi Ranch [Rancho Valle de San Felipe] and from there on to Warner the road ran through a better country for cattle. Finally we reached Warner Ranch and it looked good to us and I have no doubt our horses and cattle enjoyed the sight of it as much as we did. The grass was six to eight inches high and as green as a wheat field all over the ranch, which covers about 50,000 acres.

We had been about two months and ten days on the trail since we left the Empire Ranch. There was not a man sick on the trip that I remember. We had slept on the ground all the way except at Yuma for a few nights when our blankets were in the wagon across the river. Our men had been loyal and cheerful all the time and I am glad to have all them share with Tom Turner and myself in the success of our drive. After we reached Warner, the Justice of the Peace sent for men and inquired about the trouble at Carrizo Creek. I told him what I saw just as I have related it in this diary, he then told me that the officers were out of their jurisdiction in California as they had no papers from the California Governor at that time, but I believed they obtained them later.

We had to hold the herd for a few days until they were counted and received. Most of our men were at liberty and we all went to the Warner Hot Springs and took baths which all enjoyed. The Indian women seemed to be always washing clothes and our men would join the group and wash their own and sometimes borrow the soap from the Indian girls. There was a good deal of laughing and joking in Spanish during the performance. The water was as it comes out of the ground hot enough to cook an egg. Close by and running parallel to it is a stream of clear cold water.

The San Luis Rey River rises on the Warner Ranch and there are large meadows and several lakes as well as beautiful live oaks on the foothills of the mountains that surround the ranch. Mrs. Helen Hunt Jackson spent some time here and at Temecula gathering data for her celebrated novel, "Ramona." Very soon all the cowboys were sent to Los Angeles where they remained for a few days to see the sights of the largest city they had ever visited, but after a short time they said their legs and feet were sore from walking and that they were all right on horseback but no good on foot, so we shipped them back to Tucson and the ranch.

A short time after our return, a meeting of cattlemen was called at the Palace Hotel (now the Occidental) then owned by Marsh & Driscoll who were at that time among the largest cattle owners in Arizona. The object of the meeting was to consider the matter of establishing a safe trail from here to California for cattle. From our experience I was able to make some suggestions, viz: To build a flat boat to ferry cattle across the Colorado River. To clear out the wells at the old stage stations on the Colorado Desert and put in tanks and watering troughs at each of them and if necessary to dig or drill more wells. Without delay all the money necessary for this work was subscribed.

The Southern Pacific Railroad Company when they heard of the proposed meeting asked permission to send a representative and the cattle association notified the company that the cattlemen would be pleased to have them do so. Therefore the S.P. agent at Tucson was present. The meeting then adjourned to meet at the Hotel Bar where they found that the bartender was absent. At once they saw the chance to have some fun at the expense of Mr. Marsh who had assumed his job. Every man agreed to ask for a different kind of mixed drink which they knew the old man could not make. We all lined up at the bar and proceeded to call for various drinks we liked best. Mine Host, March, looked along the bar at our smiling faces, stuttered a little and then said, "Damn it, boys, I can't make those things, take it straight on me." We did not refuse his kind invitation and then took a few more on ourselves and on each other and departed.

Soon after our cattle meeting, we received an official letter from the S. P. Company at the Empire Ranch saying that if we would make no more drives, the old freight rate would be restored on stock cattle. The company kept its promise and it held for many years. Therefore the trail improvements were never made.

———————

About the Author

Edward "Ned" L. Vail was born September 19, 1849 in Liverpool, Nova Scotia, Canada, the eldest son of Mahlon and Elizabeth Boyle Vail. He grew up in New Jersey with his six siblings. His younger brother, Walter L. Vail persuaded Edward to come to Arizona in 1879 to join him in his ranching and mining ventures. Walter and two partners had established the Empire Ranch in 1876 and had begun the development of the Total Wreck silver mine.

Upon his arrival in Arizona Ned became the assayer of the Total Wreck Mine and later purchased and managed the Rosemont Ranch on the east slope of the Santa Rita Mountains. He participated actively in Vail family ranching operations in Arizona and California throughout his life.

A staunch Republican, Ned was a member and chair of the Pima County Board of Supervisors and served as county treasurer. He belonged to the Old Pueblo Club, which provided a meeting place for business and professional men in Tucson. He supported the Arizona Pioneer Historical Society and served as its president in 1927.

In his later years Vail began to write about his experiences in early Arizona, many of which were published in local newspapers, including the "Diary of a Desert Trail." A lifelong bachelor, he was fondly known by his nieces and nephews as "Tio." He died at the age of 87 on October 14, 1936 in Tucson.

About the Empire Ranch Foundation

Empire Land and Cattle Co. check dated June 17, 1884. ERF archives

The Empire Ranch continues as a working cattle ranch today. The Vail (1876-1928) and Boice (1928-1969) families owned it for over 90 years. Between 1969 and 1988 the Empire Ranch was owned by two private corporations which continued ranching under lease arrangements with the Boice and Donaldson families. In 1988, with public support for preserving the ranch and its grasslands from possible development, a series of land exchanges put the property into public ownership under the administration of the Bureau of Land Management (BLM). The original ranch properties are now within the BLM's Las Cienegas National Conservation Area.

In 1997, a group of private citizens, working in partnership with the BLM, formed the Empire Ranch Foundation (ERF) as a volunteer 501(c)(3) charitable organization, dedicated to preserving and interpreting the Empire Ranch historic buildings and surrounding landscape for future generations. The mission of ERF is: To protect, restore and sustain the Empire Ranch historical buildings and landscape as an outstanding western heritage education center. More information is available at our website: www.empireranchfoundation.org.